"Hey Ranger!"

Kids Ask Questions About
Yellowstone National Park

Kim Williams Justesen

Illustrated by Judy Newhouse

FALCON GUIDE®

GUILFORD, CONNECTICUT
HELENA, MONTANA
AN IMPRINT OF THE GLOBE PEQUOT PRESS

With special thanks to the wonderful and dedicated rangers who helped make this book possible. Thanks also to my family for their support and encouragement and to my darling sister who dared to ask where she could get a massage in the park.

Introduction

Each year, millions of people visit America's national parks. They come to see the many different natural wonders across our country and to learn more about what makes our country unique. Thousands of park rangers help visitors from around the world understand and enjoy all the great sights in our parks. They manage the resources of the parks, keep visitors safe, and answer questions that tourists ask.

Whether the question is great or goofy, the ranger's job is to treat each visitor with respect and handle each question with a straight face. Rangers have heard it all, but they remain friendly and helpful, even if they have answered the same question one hundred times or more that day.

Rangers live in the parks where they work. When they talk about the park, they are also talking about their home. But while rangers live and work in the national parks, the parks belong to the American people. These lands were set aside to guard their special nature and to protect them for future generations.

The most popular park, and the oldest, is Yellowstone National Park. It was the first national park in the world. It is known for its amazing geysers and abundant wildlife. For more than 125 years, visitors have been drawn to the natural wonders found here. They come to see all the different animals—the grizzly bears, black bears, elk, deer, moose, buffalo, pelicans, eagles, and more. They also come to see the boiling mud pots, the Upper and Lower Falls of Yellowstone River, the steaming hot pools, and of course, Old Faithful geyser. It is the mix of these different and interesting sights that keeps people coming back to Yellowstone year after year. It is also what draws thousands of new visitors each year.

Some visitors to Yellowstone know very little about the history, geology, and ecology of the park. This book looks at some of the interesting, funny, and sometimes off-the-wall questions that visitors ask. The answers come straight from the rangers.

Where did Yellowstone come from?

Yellowstone is in the northwest corner of Wyoming and the southwest corner of Montana. About 640,000 years ago a giant volcano erupted. It covered a huge area of the western United States and part of Mexico with a thick layer of ash. It left behind a caldera—a big bowl of geothermal activity where the heat from inside the earth shows itself—30 miles wide and 45 miles long. Today we can still see the geothermal features, such as the geysers, steam vents, mud pots, and hot pools.

How old is Yellowstone?

If you go back to the volcano that erupted and created the Yellowstone area, it's about 640,000 years old. If you go back to when the first people arrived in the area, it's about 11,000 years old. But if you count only the years it has been a national park, it's much younger. In 1872 President Ulysses S. Grant signed into law legislation to protect nearly two million acres of land "lying near the headwaters of the Yellowstone River . . . for the benefit and enjoyment of the people."

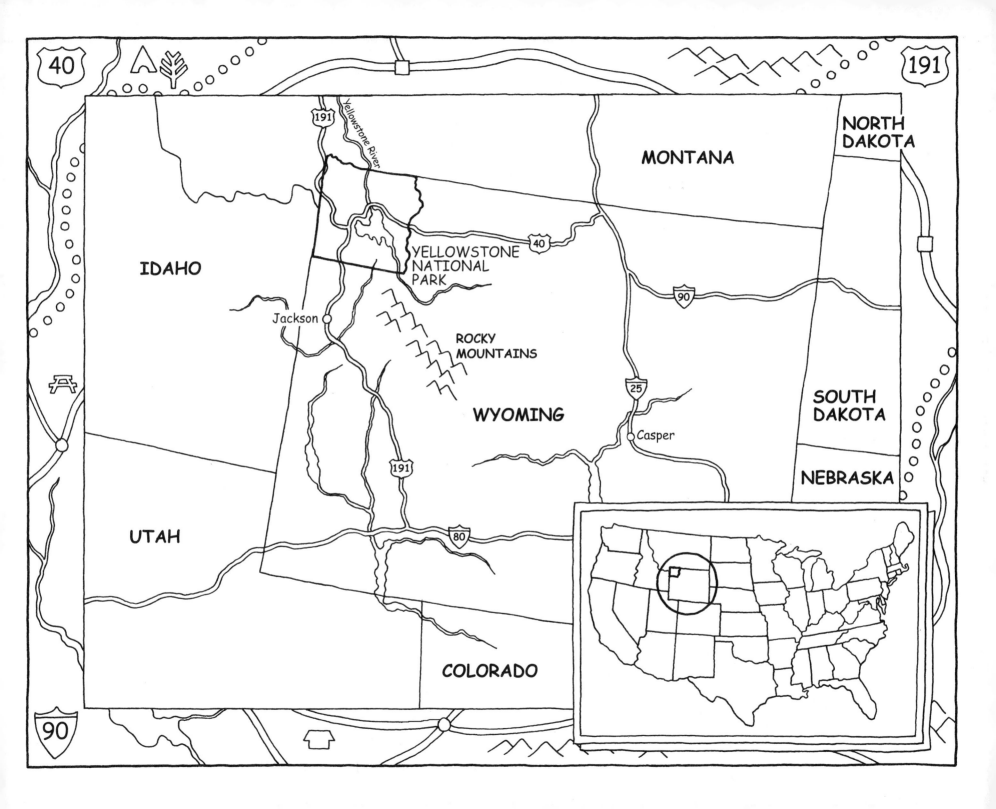

Was there much damage to the park when the volcano erupted?

The volcano erupted hundreds of thousands of years ago, before the park existed. There wouldn't even be a Yellowstone National Park today if that volcano hadn't erupted. Sometimes people think the volcano erupted just recently. Rangers are asked this question all the time.

Will the volcano erupt again?

No one can predict when another major geologic event might take place. Each day dozens of small earthquakes are measured with the seismic equipment that's kept in the Old Faithful visitor center. These small tremors are signs of the area's restlessness.

In 1959 an earthquake of 7.5 magnitude—which is really big and powerful—struck just outside the park's west entrance. This giant quake sent a 20-foot-high wall of water charging down through Madison Canyon. It caused a 7,600-foot-high mountain to collapse, and it killed several people. This earthquake also caused changes to geysers and hot springs. Even as big as the quake was, it was small compared to the volcano.

Who was the first person in Yellowstone?

Humans have been in Yellowstone for about 11,000 years. We don't know much about these early people, but we know that ancestors of Native American peoples lived here or visited the area for thousands of years after these first people arrived. There was plenty of game to hunt, such as elk, deer, and buffalo.

Evidence of early Native Americans has been found throughout the park. Arrowheads and spear points show researchers that hunting the many animals in the area was what drew these people to Yellowstone. They stayed in the area until the end of the nineteenth century.

In 1806 some members of the Lewis and Clark Expedition came very close to where the park is now. Later, a member of the expedition explored the area. His name was John Colter. He joined the Missouri Fur Trading Company and returned to the Yellowstone area to hunt for beaver and other valuable furs. Colter is believed to be the first white man to see Yellowstone Lake and to visit some of the hot springs.

Who owns all the great buildings and houses?
Can I build my house here, too?

The U.S. Army built most of the houses and buildings around Mammoth Hot Springs between 1891 and 1913. The original set of buildings was part of Fort Yellowstone. They were used when the army oversaw the operation of the park. Today these buildings are used as the administration buildings for the park and as housing for park employees. In order to protect the heritage and history of the park, there are no privately owned buildings in Yellowstone. So although the park belongs to the American people, you can't build your home here.

Only 3 percent of the almost two million acres that make up Yellowstone is actually developed. That includes all the roads, buildings, paths, and walkways.

Why aren't there more paths and walkways? Why don't you make it easier to get to some areas of the park?

Only 5 percent of visitors go farther than the boardwalks to hike the trails or visit more remote sites. But unlike a city park, a national park is a wilderness. It is nature at its most wild, and that means it can be dangerous. This is especially true in Yellowstone. Geothermal features are everywhere, and you can't always see them. In some places the thin crust of the earth can be easily broken, and directly underneath lies 190-degree water. That's hot enough to seriously injure or kill a human being.

There are other dangers, too. Grizzly bears, buffalo, elk, moose, and black bears will attack humans if they feel threatened or are frightened by an unexpected hiker.

For all the dangers in Yellowstone, there are still some very fragile places. These areas need to be protected from humans. Careless hikers who stray from the paths can damage areas beyond repair. Yellowstone is a beautiful place, but that beauty must be treated with respect.

My family and I are here only for the afternoon. Which road would be the fastest to see the park?

Yellowstone National Park covers two million acres of land. That's the size of Delaware and Rhode Island put together! No matter which road you take through the park, if you're in a hurry you will miss a lot. Animals sometimes use the roads, too. Each year elk, buffalo, wolves, and other animals are injured or killed by drivers who are in a hurry. Buffalo often move onto the road and stay there. That means you can only go as fast as the buffalo will let you.

In order to see some of the most remarkable parts of the park, you have to leave the main road, park your car, and get out and walk. If you are in a hurry you will miss some of the most incredible scenery in America.

Why can't we swim in the hot springs?

The hot springs in Yellowstone are not like a hot tub where the temperature is usually no more than 101 degrees Fahrenheit. The water in the hot springs in Yellowstone can be as hot as 190 degrees Fahrenheit. That means it can cook your dinner—or it can cook you!

Can we fix our dinner in a hot spring?

The hot springs are definitely hot enough to cook food, but you probably don't want to do that. Tests of the water in the springs show that there are some dangerous things in the water, including arsenic, which is a poison, and heavy metals.

Why are the hot springs, like Mammoth, drying up?

The springs are not drying up, they just change every once in a while. As the water from the spring flows to the surface, it leaves mineral deposits behind. As those deposits build up, they force the water to flow around them or they block the flow of water at that spot. That means the water has to find a new outlet, which changes the appearance of a hot spring from time to time.

What time do you let the animals out for feeding?

There are some people, believe it or not, who think that Yellowstone is like a zoo. The truth is, when you visit Yellowstone, you are visiting the animals in their homes. They eat when it is natural to them, and they are not kept in cages until it is time to eat. The best time to see animals eating is early in the morning before sunrise or at dusk as the sun is setting. A ranger can tell you where different animals have been seen enjoying breakfast and dinner.

Why do you let so many wild animals run loose in the park?

The animals are not kept in cages or fed on a schedule. They live in Yellowstone. They are wild animals living in the wilderness. This area is the natural home to bears, moose, deer, eagles, pelicans, buffalo, elk, raccoons, skunks, chipmunks, squirrels, and many others.

How old do deer have to be before they turn into elk?

Deer and elk, although they sort of look alike, are two different animals. While they both have antlers and a similar body type, elk are bigger than deer. Elk also make a distinctive sound called bugling, which sounds similar to a trumpet. Elk antlers are large, with broad, flat parts rimmed with little, pointy spines. Deer have smaller antlers that grow in long, slender spikes.

When do horns turn into antlers?

There is a difference between horns and antlers, and one does not turn into the other. Horns are permanent. They stay attached to an animal's skull even when they die. Horns are made of keratin, a type of protein. This is what your fingernails are made of. Antlers are made of a mineral called calcium carbonate, which is what your bones are made of. Unlike horns, antlers are not permanent. They fall off each year in the spring and grow back during the year. In the fall elk rattle their antlers together like swords as a way to intimidate other bull elk (males) and to attract cow elk (females).

How do you tell the buffalo from the bison?

You probably already know the answer to this one, but some people really can't tell the difference. Of course *buffalo* and *bison* are two different words for the same animal—that big, brown, fuzzy animal that wanders around the park and occasionally causes traffic jams.

Why do you let the buffalo dig up the grass and make those big dirt patches?

Those dirt patches are called wallows. They are good for the buffalo and good for the park. When buffalo roll around in the dirt it's like they are taking a bath. This "bath" cleans insects off their hides and removes burrs and seeds from their fur. The dirt wallows created by the buffalo help the water in Yellowstone, too. They work like a water filter, getting fresh water to the roots of the plants and trees. This helps the plants, which in turn helps the environment.

Why can't we feed or ride the animals?

Buffalo may look cute and cuddly, but they weigh more than a ton and have sharp horns. Buffalo can run up to 40 miles per hour, and people gored by their horns have been seriously injured and even killed. Elk can charge at speeds up to 50 miles per hour. They have been known to knock over visitors with their large antlers and kick them with their strong hooves. Moose can also knock people over, stomp on them if they get too close, and even kill them with their powerful legs.

For a long time people fed the bears bread, marshmallows, or other food from their car windows. After many years of being fed by humans, raiding park garbage dumps, and learning to be dependent on people for food, the bears became more and more aggressive, injured visitors, and became unhealthy and uncooperative.

Scientists and rangers now know that bears require protein from animals, wild berries, and nuts. Hunting and killing their own food helps keep bears healthier and keeps them from being tempted by human food.

Why did you bring wolves to the park? Won't they mess everything up?

Wolves were a part of Yellowstone long before people arrived on the scene. Scientists have found fossilized bones of prehistoric wolves throughout the park. Although wolves existed in the park for many years, they were hunted across the United States, including in Yellowstone, almost to extinction. Without the wolf, other animal populations such as deer, elk, beaver, and others, became overabundant. It was left to park rangers to thin overgrown herds. In 1995 Yellowstone again had wolves within its boundaries. The original group, called the Druid Peak pack, has gone on to thrive and raise new generations that have formed more packs in the park. The return of the wolves has meant a return to the natural balance between predators and herds. The wolves have been good for the park in other ways, too. In fact, many visitors come to Yellowstone just to see the wolves.

I don't want to touch the animals, I just want to take pictures. Why can't I get out of my car?

Almost every animal in the park is faster than you are, and quite a few of them are stronger than you are. Taking pictures is fine if you're pulling your car over in a turnout, and if you are observing the rules of keeping a safe distance from the animals. If you want a picture of a bear, stay in your car or use a telephoto lens on your camera. You should never be closer than 200 yards to a bear—no matter what. If rangers ask you to stay in your car or to get back in your car when looking at animals, you should definitely do it.

What animals are here that we can't see?

Moose are often hard to see because they are pretty reclusive animals. They prefer swampy, wet areas, and they live in smaller groups than elk and deer do. Beaver are difficult to see because they do their work in streams and creeks, and they stay away from humans. There are bats and owls that come out only at night.

It takes sharp eyes to see some of the animals, but rangers will tell you the best places to look. Some animals that used to live in Yellowstone but that you won't see anymore are wooly mammoths, trilobites, giant sloths, and prehistoric camels.

What's with all the burned trees?
Why do rangers let so much of the park burn?

Every once in a while, a fire burns in the park and leaves behind the trunks of burned trees. For many years fires were put out as quickly as possible. This left debris that became fuel and ignited other fires.

The largest fire in recent history happened in 1988. During that summer nearly 794,000 acres, or 36 percent of the park, were damaged. Firefighters were able to get it under control before fire reached any buildings. Much of the park that burned has grown back, but there are markers that show where the new growth areas are.

Since then the National Park Service has implemented a policy of natural fire management. In other words, a fire is allowed to burn itself out with little or no human involvement. Rangers have learned a lot about the importance of fires and fire ecology. For example, the seeds of the lodgepole pine are tucked inside a pinecone that can be opened only by the heat of a fire. Without fire, the seeds are unable to grow into a new tree.

Why don't they take the dead trees out?

As with most things, Mother Nature does the best job of management. The trees that remain standing, even though they are burned and dead, provide homes for animals such as bats and squirrels, for insects, and for small rodents. They are part of the natural state of the forest that makes up much of Yellowstone.

Some of the dead trees were not killed by fire but by natural processes that occur in the park. The mineral hot springs and steam vents sometimes shift their locations. Runoff from the springs flows in a new direction, and sometimes that means it flows in the direction of trees. Over time, a tree can be caught by this shifting flow of hot water and gradually die or become covered in mineral deposits. Not only does nature take care of the problem, but it would be very dangerous for a ranger to remove a tree that has been killed by a hot spring.

But the burned trees are so ugly.
Can't rangers remove them once they are down?

In time the tree will fall on its own and begin to decay. This provides food for some insects and animals, as well as nourishment for the soil. This helps other trees and plants to grow, continuing the cycle of nature.

How do you get the trees planted so evenly?

When a tree reseeds, whether it is after a fire or in the spring when the snow melts, it has to have certain things to grow. It needs good soil, sunlight, and water. In order to get enough of each of these things, there has to be the right amount of spacing between the new tree and other trees or plants around it. If there isn't enough sunlight, the tree won't grow. If the seed lands in the shadow of another tree, it doesn't have a good chance of getting very big.

Animals such as squirrels, mice, and birds also spread seeds. This helps give new trees a better chance at getting the sunshine and water they need. Rangers do not come in and plant trees, nor do they hire anyone to plant them. That's what makes Yellowstone so beautiful—nature does all the work.

I saw some pretty flowers and I wanted to pick some to take with me. Why can't I?

Lots of interesting and beautiful flowers grow in Yellowstone. Monkshood flowers grow in the wet, marshy areas. In the wooded areas there are wild strawberries, primrose, sagebrush, Indian paintbrush, and many more. However, with millions of visitors each year, imagine what would happen to Yellowstone if everyone took something, even just a few flowers. We would not have beautiful flowers to look at. Over time Yellowstone would be stripped bare.

Elk, moose, deer, and buffalo eat many of Yellowstone's plants and flowers. If tourists picked too many flowers in the park, it could mean a shortage of food for the animals.

About Park Rangers

Park rangers come in all ages, colors, shapes, and sizes. They are men and women who care about our environment and enjoy working with people. They provide information, lead campfire talks on special topics, lead visitors on guided hikes, and oversee the day-to-day operations of the park. They also gather scientific information and create informational resources such as brochures or signs.

For visitors who have a problem, such as a car accident or something stolen, park rangers are the same as police officers. They take reports, help manage traffic, work like detectives, and can even arrest people. Rangers also lead Junior Ranger programs, which give kids an opportunity to learn more about the place they are visiting.

Rangers help keep visitors safe and protect the wildlife and the environment in the park. They supervise campgrounds, find firewood for campers, help fight small fires, and make sure campers follow safe-camping rules. This is especially important in Yellowstone where bears live.

Gift certificate

$20

slcroma.com

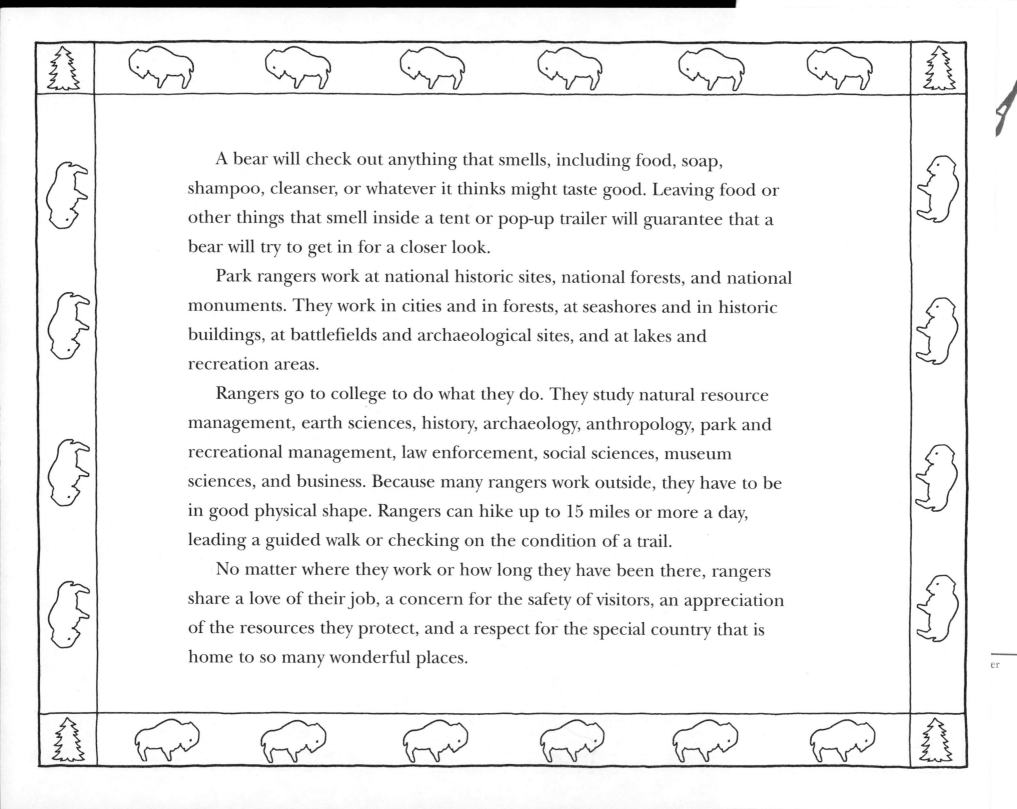

A bear will check out anything that smells, including food, soap, shampoo, cleanser, or whatever it thinks might taste good. Leaving food or other things that smell inside a tent or pop-up trailer will guarantee that a bear will try to get in for a closer look.

Park rangers work at national historic sites, national forests, and national monuments. They work in cities and in forests, at seashores and in historic buildings, at battlefields and archaeological sites, and at lakes and recreation areas.

Rangers go to college to do what they do. They study natural resource management, earth sciences, history, archaeology, anthropology, park and recreational management, law enforcement, social sciences, museum sciences, and business. Because many rangers work outside, they have to be in good physical shape. Rangers can hike up to 15 miles or more a day, leading a guided walk or checking on the condition of a trail.

No matter where they work or how long they have been there, rangers share a love of their job, a concern for the safety of visitors, an appreciation of the resources they protect, and a respect for the special country that is home to so many wonderful places.

NATIONAL
PARK
SERVICE

About the Author

Kim Williams Justesen lives with her husband, three children, two cats, and one dog in their home in Sandy, Utah. Kim earned her bachelors degree in English from Westminster College of Salt Lake City and her masters in writing for children from Vermont College in Montpelier. Besides camping and hiking in our national parks, Kim enjoys knitting, crocheting, and reading. In addition to writing, she teaches English at a small, private college in Salt Lake City.

About the Artist

Illustrator Judy Newhouse is a graduate of Moore College of Art in Pennsylvania. Her work ranges from cartoons to precise medical drawings. She lives with her artist husband in a log house in Chester Springs, Pennsylvania. When not illustrating books, Judy loves to garden, cook, travel, and visit her daughter, an actor in New York City.